TeNNiS iN VeNice

Pam Scheunemann

Consulting Editor, Diane Craig, M.A./Reading Specialist

Published by ABDO Publishing Company, 4940 Viking Drive, Edina, Minnesota 55435.

Printed in the United States.

Credits
Edited by: Pam Price
Curriculum Coordinator: Nancy Tuminelly
Cover and Interior Design and Production: Mighty Media
Photo Credits: BananaStock Ltd., Eyewire Images, Hemera, Image Source, PhotoDisc, Rubberball Productions, Stockbyte, Thinkstock

Library of Congress Cataloging-in-Publication Data

Scheunemann, Pam, 1955-
    Tennis in Venice / Pam Scheunemann.
        p. cm. -- (Rhyme time)
    Includes index.
    ISBN 1-59197-818-1 (hardcover)
    ISBN 1-59197-924-2 (paperback)
    1. English language--Rhyme--Juvenile literature. I. Title. II. Rhyme time (ABDO Publishing Company)

    PE1517.S46 2004
    428.1'3--dc22
                                                                    2004049108

SandCastle™ books are created by a professional team of educators, reading specialists, and content developers around five essential components that include phonemic awareness, phonics, vocabulary, text comprehension, and fluency. All books are written, reviewed, and leveled for guided reading, early intervention reading, and Accelerated Reader® programs and designed for use in shared, guided, and independent reading and writing activities to support a balanced approach to literacy instruction.

Let Us Know

After reading the book, SandCastle would like you to tell us your stories about reading. What is your favorite page? Was there something hard that you needed help with? Share the ups and downs of learning to read. We want to hear from you! To get posted on the ABDO Publishing Company Web site, send us e-mail at:

sandcastle@abdopub.com

SandCastle Level: Fluent

Words that rhyme do not have to be spelled the same. These words rhyme with each other:

bliss
notice
hiss
practice
iris
Swiss
kiss
tennis
miss
this

Maya thinks going down the slide is **bliss**.

This purple and yellow flower is an iris.

Trevor pets the kitten gently so it won't scratch and **hiss**.

Gabriela raised her hand so the teacher would **notice**.

Jared and Angela each give their mom a **kiss**.

The softball team meets once a week to **practice**.

Nathaniel hopes he won't swing and miss.

Whitney's family is playing table tennis.

At the party, Courtney and Jade had sandwiches made with pastrami and **Swiss** cheese.

Chase brought his mom breakfast and said, "I hope you like this."

Tennis in Venice

Chris liked
to play tennis.

He played
everywhere,
from New York
to Venice.

BIG TENNIS
MATCH
Chris vs. Swiss
Next Saturday

One day Chris
got a game notice.

He was going to play the Swiss.

He called to tell
his friend Iris.

Hey, Iris! Please come watch me play the Swiss.

This was a match
she could not miss.

Chris worked hard at his practice.

Then he beat the Swiss
and was full of bliss.

Rhyming Riddle

What do you call the rehearsal of a snake sound?

Practice hiss

Glossary

bliss. complete happiness

Swiss. of or relating to the country of
Switzerland or its people

table tennis. a game played by two or four
players who use wooden paddles to hit a
ball over a net that is streched across a
table

tennis. a game played by two or four
players who use rackets to hit a ball over
a net

Venice. a city in Italy that is known for its
canals

About SandCastle™

A professional team of educators, reading specialists, and content developers created the SandCastle™ series to support young readers as they develop reading skills and strategies and increase their general knowledge. The SandCastle™ series has four levels that correspond to early literacy development in young children. The levels are provided to help teachers and parents select the appropriate books for young readers.

Emerging Readers
(no flags)

Beginning Readers
(1 flag)

Transitional Readers
(2 flags)

Fluent Readers
(3 flags)

These levels are meant only as a guide. All levels are subject to change.

To see a complete list of SandCastle™ books and other nonfiction titles from ABDO Publishing Company, visit www.abdopub.com or contact us at:
4940 Viking Drive, Edina, Minnesota 55435 • 1-800-800-1312 • fax: 1-952-831-1632